FOREIGN PARK

FOREIGN PARK

JEFF STEUDEL

ANVIL PRESS / VANCOUVER

Anvil Press Publishers Inc.
P.O. Box 3008, Main Post Office
Vancouver, B.C. V6B 3X5 CANADA
www.anvilpress.com

Library and Archives Canada Cataloguing in Publication

Steudel, Jeff, 1966–, author
Foreign park / Jeff Steudel.

Poems.
ISBN 978-1-77214-015-6 (pbk.)

I. Title.

PS8637.T48434F67 2015   C811'.6   C2015-901623-1

Cover design by Rayola Graphic
Cover image: Mount Robson postcard image courtesy of *Peel's Prairie Provinces*, a digital initiative of the University of Alberta Libraries. peel.library.ualberta.ca
Author photo by Aaron Aubrey
Interior by HeimatHouse
Represented in Canada by the Publishers Group Canada
Distributed by Raincoast Books

The publisher gratefully acknowledges the financial assistance of the Canada Council for the Arts, the Canada Book Fund, and the Province of British Columbia through the B.C. Arts Council and the Book Publishing Tax Credit.

For Susan, Chris and Wil

Contents

AFTER HOPE

MOUTH

"…we cannot draw a line that delineates where air ends and we begin because air is in us, fused to our lungs and circulates in our bloodstream. We are air."

—David Suzuki, *The Legacy*

"Without the river no one is married."

—Sina Queyras, *Lemon Hound*

HEADWATERS

A bee lands on the dash. Not long ago
we prepared for snowstorms. Now glaciers seep
into waterfalls. Runnels run rampant. Roots
loosen and rocks tumble as if from goats' eyes
to kicking horses. Somewhere in the pine,
a grizzly's hunger rouses. Such beauty exists
in alluvium and saplings sprouting new languages
through the road sand on the cut. We hear that
a mudslide has closed the next pass. Water
rises like a rooster's tail up and out of the ditch.
I park the car at the river's edge. You say, Nature
could take it all back. I say, Your eyes are prairie.
The poplars sway chartreuse, lime. The paper cup
of wine balances on your knee. I spread butter
onto the rye. The river a rush of whispers,
we have no need.

READING RILKE ON DOG MOUNTAIN

I know the sound letting go makes.
I see it still: Two ravens tap beaks and bray
like dry kisses until one springs off the snowdrift.
Its heavy whir sets air in motion.

So soon, it glides like a black angel tilting
in the wind's tuneless portamento. It vanishes
beyond the tall hemlock on the trail
where I lean onto the wide clefts of bark

and rest on the twin trunk that grew
to the deep bend of an S-curve. I don't know
how much farther to climb, so I stay
until I have to decide. The second

bird has left the clearing, and yet I hear
their faint calls like half-blown watery whistles
breaking the mountain stillness as I turn
the page back to "In a Foreign Park."

GUARDING THE CREATION MYTH

I am admiring *The Raven and the First Men*
from the tall chair vacated by the security guard
when I think, Raven is watching me. Natural light
brightens his crown, a bit of wing. As I shift,
the flash off the spotlight catches my eye. Alone
in the rotunda, I cross my arms and remember
how I thought the *Mona Lisa* was priceless. Raven
cannot follow my eyes, as I read that Erickson
designed the room around a gun turret. The creation
was set onto the defence point. Japanese and German
tourists now shoot photographs here on what was
Musqueam land. The Saanich poet cursed and wept
when he saw his grandparents' grave box, its serpent's
two heads preserved. I imagine my own grandparents
alive. How do we belong to the past?

                                        A fledgling
pecks on the concrete steps outside the window.
A man, cradling an infant in a chest-carrier, points
to one of the first men. His daughter asks why
there is no clam gut. She fingers a design in the sand
surrounding the sculpture. I realize how massive
Raven is compared to the clam. I hop off the chair.
The first men look like children. What did Raven say
to get them out? Where are the women? The guard
returns. I say, "Thank you." I buy a Frog T-shirt
at the gift shop. Outside, I walk among the cedars.
So many birds.

HORNBY ISLAND VACATION

In a yellow field that slopes to the ocean
and belongs to the farmer
who made his fortune
in the parking lot business,
I watch the dragonflies
sell the sound of electric
crimped air, their glide
uneasy, even clumsy
as they sputter and fall
until double-winged charges
prop up their flight paths; surely
they must go broke.
The bee's golden parcels:
drop-off, pickup;
the wasp's tenacity
around the peach pie—
and me, knowing I will soon
leave this small economy
when September comes,
top-heavy and buzzing,
to get back to work.

RECIPE

The laundry sink overflowing with hockey
equipment, robots on the floor, we cook later
these days to saxophones like incandescent bulbs
lighting snooker tables in a basement pool hall.
We read out the ingredients and improvise:
plums and brandy for lemon; coriander, cumin,
and cayenne for a curry. Chorizo, garlic, cream,
and chives already on the stovetop, I read out
the steps. You flip the snapper. The steam rises
into the hood fan. I get mint from the garden.
Is this sex?   I read...   You...
          Yes dear...
read. Dear?   Yes. Soft lips of oysters
on the countertop. I cup your nipples. Bounce.

GOOD LIGHT

Comes with shadows. There are cherry branches
on this page, their serrated leaves dulled, the edges
lost. Through the tall maple, circles of sunlight shine
kaleidoscopic on the long, dry grass. The woodshed
is heaped in hops. Like me. The old blue paint is
chipped on the window frame around four panes
caked with resin—dirty like the years of home
renovation when we all slept in the same small
basement room. In the dust and in the sun, things
take new shapes. A fern touches a cedar bough
like I want to touch you. Wings open. Limelight
glows through new growth of red-spine leaves
over the cabin door. To one side of this lawn chair,
ants climb into pine cones, over yellow moss and up
blades of grass. To the other, the lost light of us.
And though the eastern sky still holds—blue, a wisp
of cirrus—and the sinking sun flashes its finale
on the aluminum chimney cap, nothing is brighter
than the sound of you chopping tomatoes in the kitchen.

POSSUM

After my nap, I helped my neighbours
carry tent poles and tarps to the peacock shed.
"Dead a week?" I asked. "Nothing's still
eating that," said Stevie. "What a strange place
to die," said Mia. The possum's fallen face
flat on a mop handle. An empty plastic cup
inches from its rotten chalk-like teeth.

Had the peacocks found their python-
snagging ways, while the possum lapped up
a leftover Mojito from Friday night's bonfire?
Or was it Rusty Ham, the cat I mistook
for a cougar on the pergola—his *mea culpa*
before being relocated to the city? Maybe,
after gorging on all my coffee filters mixed
into the compost, the possum lay down
its racing heart in the heat wave of summer.

When Mia and Stevie left to unload
the rest of the trade stand into the house,
I rocked the carcass onto a spade, held up
its limp tail with a broom and carried it
to the anthill behind the vacant chicken coop.
Sometime later I would examine it for signs
of fracture. The only sure thing that day,
there would be no more sleep.

No more sleep, even though the flies
had settled, and the long, dry grass was still.
The thrushes were silent. The evening
sky a deep blue. I did my best to become
comfortable in the stasis, but a waft of warm wind
arrived from the east. I stood up and raised
my arms to it. It vanished. When I lay down,
it came once more, brief and light.

DEDICATION

The chemo is poison. Your face ruddy,
alcoholic, but your blue eyes are yours.
You tell me the two-week rotation ends
in vomit. Sleep. Maybe some television. Still
you take the kids to school, play early Beatles'
songs with the band. You've organized this party.
The beer in coolers, bins full of empties.
Our children play their own games with water.
There are mustards. Sliced ham. Sushi trays.
On the porch, people discuss whether love
should have need. By eight, you are tired, stay
in your chair for longer, your voice the same
as it has always been. Measured. You rise,
"The Magician will be here shortly."

.

CONFLUENCE

The river takes so much water in and through
this canyon that is the V in valley and the falling
rock in steep. I say, Imagine if we harnessed
all that power. The pressure in a penstock pushes
turbines. Magnets circling coils move free
electrons into wires that link up over long distances
and reach the yellow light bulb above the glass of water
on a desk. You say, Think of the salmon.
After we leave, the two rivers will still merge
into a mud of eddies that turns to flow, and we
will continue to be connected because of our time
together. You've gone up ahead. Some sage
brush blows by a burned-down campfire, and off
the low bank of this sandy shoal, the water
around my foot is as calm as
a shallow pool.

EVAPORATION

The month of my childhood in hospital
remains in the plastic croup tent where

I watched the freckled boy in the next bed
eat bananas. He would run from the nurses

who'd chase him to the elevator and tie him
to a wheelchair. Hurting too, he'd pull his shirt

overhead like a brown-lipped snail. A nurse
said he pulled out my tubes. I don't remember,

not now. Only the one tube a doctor forced
into my nose. How I cried all wet and steam,

not like it was, but how I might remember
my mother's soft, dry hand on my forehead.

A BRANCH OF BEES

The static boiled over *Moonlight Sonata*,
while my father and I drove up the mountain
to check on the hive. After a slow turn,
the valley's haze, the winding Fraser
a turn after that. He told me about the sturgeon
found alive in the furrow of a farmer's field
weeks after the river rose up its banks.

Up the road, his friend waved off dust
from his tennis whites. He leaned in. A laurel
leaf, pipe smoke. *The swarm is in the orchard.*

My father dipped a kerchief in kerosene,
snapped his silver lighter and blew oil-thick smoke
up the tree. He cut the buzzing branch.

As he churned, they churned.

I moved closer to his branch of bees
that trailed like a tattered flag as he walked
to the white stacks and lifted the red lid.
A bee landed in his thick black hair.
I yelled, "Be careful!" He didn't flinch.

As we merged onto the highway,
I said it was a wonder he was stung
just once. He said, "The honey'll be good."
I glanced over at his swollen eye,
and I thought of the sturgeon, if it had been
hooked often and lived, and lived on.

SHEPHERD

My ear on the pillow, your wet hair on my neck,
I haven't felt like this since I was a kid,
lying on the orange carpet, looking
at the bits of glass on the ceiling—the nights
before Christmas, the World Cup.

The lights on the sill like water droplets,
parcels wrapped in brown paper
from my grandmother in Germany.
We opened them at night
while she ate breakfast.

THE FINAL

Every weekend at his pickup soccer game,
he honours life, liberty and the right to carry
boots. And just as cleaved grass still clings
to cleats from the week before, his dreams
stay alive. His stomach tingles at the prospect
of the next cross, the next goal, unmatched
by anyone in La Liga or league: Gargantuan is
the glory of the one true meditation for him
running on grass, gravel, even snow-packed
pitches. Nothing else registers—no job, no family,
only the breakout, the tight pass. He gives,
he goes until the boil of his knackered knees
and the breath he has left is just enough
to get home, to drink a lot of beer, to recover.

AND SPHYGMOMANOMETERS

I was checking my blood pressure
in the white room where an enlarged photograph of
a sunflower field was helping me relax.

The turn of the handle, creak of the door.
My blood picked up speed: Kahn's forehead
after a goal, Rooney's after a red card.

My tall, tanned doctor said, "Let's test your monitor."
Again I wrapped the cuff. The meter cranked
and cranked—I was way too high.
"Let's compare it to the office monitor."
Air wheezed out of the bulb. I drooped
and contemplated the high numbers,
always higher than my home numbers.

Then I, the defender, dribbled up the wing, cut
to the inside and sliced the ball
to the top left corner. The forward tapped one in.
The holding-midfielder struck from thirty metres out.

My doctor whistled. He said his monitor
read twelve points lower than mine.
He told me to watch my weight. I scattered
a defence: baguettes and World Cup beer.

QUALIFYING HEAT

Blossoms burst into the snowflakes of spring.
Chain-link rings a skating rink. Marijuana wafts.
A little warmth by the water is worth the day.

The Lions beguile, but snow is a duck's wing,
pinioned wind. A woman swings her jacket as
blossoms burst into the snowflakes of spring.

Banners on buildings champion electronics, junk
food and athletes. Long lines and zip line lines.
A little warmth by the water is worth the day.

Helicopters and a jet stream. A man stretches
for a shovel in a purple pail. His toddler digs in.
Blossoms burst into the snowflakes of spring.

The willow's whip-thin branches flop like hair
on stumps. A retriever jumps. Clucks of flight.
A little warmth by the water is worth the day.

Gulls beat the crows to the crumbs every time.
Last year the lake was ice, but this year the best
blossoms burst into the snowflakes of spring.
A little warmth by the water is worth the day.

GROUND TEMPERATURES

My dream began in a park near a lake
that was fed and drained by culverts under
the fields depressed to gullies where willows
that had been pruned to stumps were beginning
to sprout again. The barn swallows circled
dogs who gave idle chase and who wagged
their frothed-out joy nonetheless. A man
who untangled a fishing line pressed a cell
to his ear with his free hand. Two women
in visors walked backwards. A deflated ball
bobbed in the yellow reeds. It was the one
frozen onto the lake in December. A shepherd
broke through the ice trying to get it. Gone.

Then late in the summer as a stretch of heat
drove me into the basement, I behaved
as predictably as another argument ending
nothing inside our hot little house of mirrors.
I unrolled the mattress and a sleeping bag
onto the floor. I opened all the windows
and the door. I had finally reached the point
where I was willing to risk burglary, even
a personal injury, to get some kind of breeze
into the house. And sure enough, sometime
during my sauna of sleep came the mercy
of pressure falling and of clouds gathering
into the glory of rain's hush onto the trees.

After many days, the little lake spilled over
willow roots, gravel paths, knolls. The old
streams thought of salmon, the deft swipe
of a bear's paw. An eagle's ink-tipped talons
stretched for you—for me. Still our fierce selves
and still together in the fading light of dusk,
we stepped from the shore into the dark water,
but we knew that everyone must swim and dream
alone. Summer's bare sun returned; it heated,
simmered and stayed. People were begging—
some of us on our knees—for a good hard rain,
so we pleased each other like a deep blown
breath, because everybody feels better after that.

THE BIG TREE

Lost its peak in '86
for the second time. Lower branches
limbed in '75. All 276 rings
of its twin cut in '54 to give the old-growth fir
a better chance. The road widened around it in '52,
paved in '84. The west woods logged '34, '54 and '79.
In 2000, people noticed its rutted trunk
leaning to the high side of the road. In the fall
of 2012, cones still dropped onto its roots;
its claw of splintered top
and whirligig of boughs way up high
still marked land to sky. Its story—
a time of larger life
now ragged in its glory.

BONSAI

He sets it on the pine sill mottled with faint rings
from the tumblers of wine. His apartment
facing the courtyard glows with Christmas lights.
So much, so little. Always
it's the smile he remembers. Quietly,
he promises the sun's shiny tangerines
on a blue plate.

HELL'S GATE

Before he got to these crushing waters,
Simon Fraser must have thought he'd
found an easy route to the ocean. Against
a tree at cliff's edge, I see the torrents:
surges of electricity. Indecision has
knocked loose my will. Lightning bolts.
A canoe washed up on the black rocks
looks like a raven's open beak. I must be
close to the spot where Fraser reached
up ladders made from twigs and poles
to the Stó:lō guides who hoisted him,
his men and his guns. Still he ignored
their advice to turn back.

THE OIL SLICK APPROACHES

A rusty trawler drifts towards shore at sunrise.
Water bottles bob by a barnacle-clad piling.

The pipeline's terminus lies beyond a dead-end
bridge by the river. A dog barks at the garbage

bag snagged in blue pine. An albatross feeds
on plastic pellets in plankton. A pickup idles

in a garage. A yelp from the back. Gulls screech
at the dumpster. The vigil is peaceful. The sun

pales behind the plumes of the refinery. Smog
of the valley. Tomato skins and a shiny dime.

Still, everybody is surprised when an otter lures
the dog to deep water and the captain is found.

FISHING WITH GEORGE

The gentle lap, the plunk
against the skiff, we sat
across from each other,
sipped beer, shared a cigarette,
and jigged buzz bombs
five reels off the bottom.

The sun burned our knees, necks,
glints of aluminum broke
water's flint glass.
An eagle guarding cedars
beyond the white rock shore
tilted its wings
to the apogee of us.

A tug. My fingers tingled.
The line split water's mercurial skin,
the bowed rod holding
the silver salmon
until it lay on its side
slapping the bilge
in the irony of air.

I had forgotten the club,
a hammer, how to kill.
You told me to grab it,
and smack it across the gunwale,
but I kicked it with my heel
until it was still.

FINN'S SLOUGH

The grey boathouses, sheds, and homes sag
towards the big mud after ten thousand or more
bleached sunrises. Then there's the rain.

For now, it's the blue Boler I'm interested in,
the one that's all sky on top and wide open ocean
on the bottom. It's next to the aquamarine

Chevy truck stuffed with tarpaulin. Flowers in
small pots sit on its big round fenders. A dented
orange wheelbarrow and blackberry bushes

under the old telephone lines. If I could, I'd call
Williams, or Steinbeck who would surely have
one "for thirst...a second one for taste" with me

on this scorching day. The old women, crouching
in the field across the road, wear white canopies
to shield themselves from the sun while they pick

broccoli. All hard work or no work. The last fishing
season lasted a day. The boards on the dock lift,
and a bench is one inch away from breaking.

And yet there is order here. So many signs: Stop.
Private. Toxic. The Dinner Plate Island School,
a green lamp directly above it. The home mid-slough

with such symmetry: moose antlers above an open,
leaded window, above an overturned metal boat
that covers a deck furnished with motors, the largest

dead centre along the railing. The whole village
rises and falls with the river. This year the salmon
forecast is outstanding. The artists inhabit. Resolute.

A HOOK IN THE EYE

The river was low. We lost two of our four sets of tackle
in the first ten minutes, so we walked around one bend after
another looking for a good spot. In the shade of a birch
a guy in a silver shirt was drinking a Colt, his line barely
in the water, his pink face and big sunken eyes as if he wasn't
supposed to be there. Around the next bend, lines stretched.
The boys ran ahead. Gutted salmon as long as my arm lay
in a small pool off a low bank. I told the boys to hold back,
but they inched toward the men who stood as little as a foot
from each other as they reeled and cast. A guy in black jeans
and a blue shirt with a green pack of King Size Export As
sticking out of his chest pocket told the boys they could take
his place. While he pulled on a smoke, their lines tangled
in the others. Then from up the bank, a skin-slicing scream
pierced me like a knife on my neck. A young Vietnamese
boy's eyelid got hooked and ripped. His father pulled it out,
picked him up and held the boy's eye closed. He ran with
his son and yelled to him, to everybody, "It's okay! It's . . . "
The screaming and the father's eyes were like something just
caught. The wiry guy who had been cooking a salmon over
an open flame and who said, "Welcome to the Gong Show"
when we arrived, was suddenly right next to the father.
"I'm parked right over there. Let's go." And they were gone.
I cut the rig off the line that I'd just tied. The King snagged
another sockeye. "God-damn luck," he said, "I want springs."
He tossed the big hook-nosed fish to the boys, who scrambled
to catch it. They scraped out its guts into the water and held it
by its ripped gills. "Keep it," he said. I told them to wrap it up.
"You leaving already?" asked the King, walking backwards,
and towards us, as he pulled another sockeye out of the river.

THE ACCIDENT

I was heading up Victoria Drive when I saw the flashing reds, and I knew. I had just heard the CBC report that the NEB gave their first green light to the Northern Gateway Pipeline. The spokesperson said, "... with alarums and excursions," and I wondered if she was referring to Macduff's reaction upon seeing Duncan's bloody corpse. Yes it was treason, and much of it against the First Nations who may now be the only hope left for the coast. I approached the accident scene in the crosswalk by the Edwardian for sale and Tutta Mia Designs. As I was forced to turn right, I saw the light green backpack—that was, I was sure—lighter than my son's, but I had to check. I ran. A woman in a geo-print dress stood apart, crying. I thought she was a witness but then I realized she had been driving the silver Honda Prelude that hit the boy who was on a stretcher and covered to his chin by a blanket with two thin red stripes near the ends—his head rounder, larger; it wasn't my son. He had the same pale skin, the same shag of blond hair. My head a hammer, I wanted to be sure I wasn't wrong. The paramedics wheeled the boy into the ambulance, and the officer asked a guy in carpenter pants if he had taken any first-aid training. The windshield was smashed but still hanging together in millions of aquamarine pieces. Then I saw it happen: The sun oblique, a young man steps off a curb, a black sneaker, earphones, the deafening shock of the impact changing the boy's life and the woman's. One moment a person could be changing gears, listening to Bizet, noticing a cyclist's skull helmet; the next... "What happened?" I asked the carpenter. "A kid was hit by a car." It was the reasonable answer to a stupid question, but I wanted to know, and to believe the kid would be alright. I drove around the block and then up the hill towards my house. I saw my son walking home in the middle of the day on the last of school. "Why are ... am I ever happy to see you," I said. "What a coincidence." "Last day," he said. The next day, I searched the papers. There was nothing except for Stephen Hume's article about the NEB's "Theatre of the Absurd." The stage for a national disaster. And now when I pass that intersection, I think of the impacts, the windshield like rough seas, the boy and the woman. The conditions.

SOUP

He melts the mountain of white butter, kills
the onions, boils and skins the field tomatoes.
He divides the garlic bulb and slices the celery
into ridged foothills. The tap water reminds him
of the mill. Sulphur and barley. The window open,
he hears the neighbour's toilet. In a dragon pot
on the back deck, the Christmas tree's red needles
have fallen. A water stain like rust. The bleach
used up, he applies a jug of detergent. He cubes
the beef from the farmer who sometimes shovels
chicken shit into the feed. Potatoes pulp, separate.
He pulverizes the cumin, goes easy on the cayenne,
turmeric and pepper. The salt box lid pops free
like the berm of the mine's tailings pond. Slurry
and slag destroy the creek. No more ladling water
with his coffee cup while fishing. No more fishing.
He pours the big pot down the drain to the river.

POSTCARD

He steps over the iridescent puddle by the white van.
The storm-drains overflow. A motorboat explodes
by the cannery. The rink's ice melts. Paint burbles
in the creek. A man accused of murder on the island
releases the hold on his scow, so does the family sailing
off the point. An expired bottle of Warfarin. Boat fuel
drizzles. Fish mill at the mouth. Fertilizers and pesticides
reach the river's plume. The horizontal stack discharges
chlorides, sulphides, copper, zinc, and arsenic. Inspectors
cattle-prodded out of the budget, heavy metal thunder.
Trucks as big as Edmontosauruses come to repair
the mine. The creeks and the rivers? The mountain is
a reflection on Berg Lake. Toxins in the glacier. Canada
is everywhere. The Fraser, the Nile, and the Gomati.

THE LOCAL SOURCE

At the Happy Market between the river
and the highway, the vendor's smile
lit up the room despite the blind hum
of fluorescence. As I set down the Evian,
he said that he'd returned from Seoul
just that morning. I said, "You must be
tired." I counted out the three dollars
and a dime that rolled until he trapped it
under his bandaged thumb. It snapped
onto the glass smeared with a wound
of fingerprints obscuring the Gold Rush
and Clover Leaf Scratch-and-Wins.
I cracked the seal, examined the faint
blue peaks, and imagined that bottle of
water's journey to the Coca-Cola cooler
in the store next to the Seymour River.
Glacial water seeped through fissures,
plastic pellets melted in molds. Together
in the dark hold of a freighter. For this.

MOUNTAIN AIR

The water in my pack, the air a wet log,
my heartbeat settled as I hiked up the trail
with the athletes and the tourists. My eyes
tuned to the cedars, the ferns. Not long
after the one-quarter mark, while I rested
on a landing, I set the nearly empty bottle
on a railing. As I tied up my new Nikes,
a cold breeze picked up. I reached back
but I missed. I turned and saw it land on
a branch, roll, and fall into a dry stream bed
littered with more bottles and a pink sandal.
I continued walking and then lumbering
and then wondering if I could stop buying
plastic altogether. How could I? I thought
of the editor I had met at the Railway Club
the night before. She told me about her trip
to Reykjavik, the plush hot-springs spas,
and the cans of pure Icelandic mountain air
for sale.

AND EVEN JUST BREATHING

Of course I was drunk. The last time on tequila. The hangover
still in me somewhere as a drinking song: If you keep doing this

to yourself, you are going to die a slow death. Many of us do.
The habits of our time. Nearly everything is for sale. Even carbon

gets credit. Cells mutate, multiply, yet we purposely kill off
lakes. This business evaporates. Protect progress, protest poisons.

Well, once I stood swaying on a street well after midnight, awake
within the air's freeze and aware of the hard, trodden snow

slick underfoot. The street lamp's orange light lit up the slow fall
of each flake during a moment of clarity. My mouth wide open,

the stillness of winter, of night, I remembered when the air hinted
of water or lilacs before I slipped and my teeth hit the curb.

ROOST

I came to expect them every evening
as I sat there reading and drinking cold beer
in the pink light or grey clouds or rain
of dusk. And while the crows flew east,
I buoyed melancholy with booze
until it froze in the cold blunt ache
of morning. Once, there in the darkness,

I awoke to a crow scraping its beak
on the gutter outside my window. I sat up
in the bird's nest of bed my wife had just left.
I'd been dreaming of the Great Horned Owl
perched on the Scotch pine down the street.
Its feathery eyelids remained closed
in a coned stillness though the crows cawed

and cawed, and cawed. I began to wonder
about their rituals and my own, so I stopped
drinking so much, and early one morning
I plotted the short route to Still Creek
where I'd heard the crows had been roosting
in the little that was left of the riparian strip
behind the big-box stores by the highway.

The next day, just before dawn, I looked
for them by a car dealership's sign that glowed
over some cottonwoods. A collective lung
of crows rose in their traffic of hunger.
I inhaled their dry-throated exultation bursting
in all directions. I am alive and ready for the day.

AFTER HOPE

Snow brightens the mountains. Large cows
mark the fields. I step out of the river.
The valley opens to the west. I smell smoke
from a campground. I have lost interest
in death. Fishermen line the northern banks
to find their own happiness. The river is
land and water. A train whistles. A skein
divides. I find a dog for sale on a dairy farm.
She runs in circles every morning. We walk
on the trails along the dike. I have time
to think. I am moving much slower
these days.

I STILL PICTURE US LIKE THAT

The past is how I think about it now, even though
we didn't talk about the future then. You know
I haven't faked things all these years. Debt was
called dividends: one day we order smoked cod
at a restaurant where the waiters wear linen suits,
the next we turn on the radio with the cassette player
taped shut. Not long ago people talked about renaming
Prince George to where-two-rivers-flow-together.
Sometimes we must name ourselves. I picture us
by the side of the road. The light snow swirling
as we taste snowflakes, breath spiraling. Of course
I am living in the past and the future, even if I'm wrong.
At the moment I don't need to know everything.

PINE CONE

On the rust-red leaves that printed the path
between roots like steps, I held up the cone

of little wings and bird claws on its open bracts.
The chance of a seed taking root? Of all mothers,

fathers, sons and daughters, the chance of us.
The kids swinging sticks; our son's faint freckles,

our younger son's hazel eyes; and you just ahead,
your slender hips brushing against waxen salal.

The thrushes stayed silent as we crashed through
the forest of low light dappling thicket and trunk.

Seeing the picture years later, I still have this
want of afternoons together and plans for night.

THE MATCH

He listened to the rain hit the shed's aluminum roof
in the distance. The time he first knew his wife,

they had huddled on a stump under trees that dripped
onto the sign, WORLD'S LARGEST SITKA. They bathed

in the cold shallow lake and then dried each other
with his red flannel shirt. The smell of campfire.

For hours they would drive on the open highways
beside clear-cuts, her foot on the dashboard, his arm

on the glass slot, and their cigarette smoke curling,
and uncurling. He breathed in deeply. On the radio

Tom Waits barked, *Blind love, stone blind love.*
All of it still inside him. He lit up in the blackout.

ILLUMINATION

I

I did not plan to walk down
to the crowded lantern festival
at sundown. I wore my red T-shirt
with a big bull on it. My wife said,
"You are unhappy." I loved how I felt
when I sang with her. A stilt-walker,
wearing green glow stick necklaces
and a ruffled white dress, danced.
Another woman drummed a shuffle.
Flickering purple lanterns drifted
across the little lake. People huddled
under blankets. Three low notes drew us
to the Mystery Tent. My wife said
that she felt no connection.

II

I collected medium-sized oysters
at low tide. The sliding door clicked
shut. My wife steamed broccoli. The kids
ran up the beach. Jalapeno peppers
spiked the chips. I drank cans of Canadian.
The Trans-Canada led to a dock. People
pushed carts to the water taxi. Lovers clung
to the sunset. Pickup trucks formed cargo lines.

The wildlife was hidden, except for the birds
and the six-gilled shark I unhooked from my line.
I swam where the moon lit the water. All of us
at the campfire, I stared back at myself.
We doused the flame and covered the smoke
with beach rocks. In the morning I pushed
them off and found some embers
still glowing.

THE KEYS

After the afternoon of snowshoeing through the slow melt
and stillness of Mount Seymour, I was walking back

to my car in the lower lot when I heard, "Idiot! You stupid
idiot!" A woman in beige ski pants and a helmet was trying

the doors on a red Chevy Blazer spewing exhaust. Behind
her stood a boy in an unzipped jacket. His hands raised

by his head as if he were warding off blows, he staggered
backwards in the big step of ski boots. I understood the anger,

but also the boy in that thin air of humiliation. Soon after
I was arrested again. This time by the sunset reflecting

off of Mount Baker's western slopes. They were the orange
and pink inside a blue flame—a beauty so far removed

from anything human, except for our ability to see it.
In the car, I listened to k.d. lang belt out *Helpless, helpless*

helpless. Her voice filled the valley, delta, ocean, sky...
And I thought of the time that I lost my parents' car keys

on the ski slopes of Mount Baker. What a coincidence
and how unbelievable that somebody found and turned in

those keys in that record year of snowfall, but it happened
and I don't even remember what my parents said or did.

EXPANDING THE COMMUNITY GARDEN

Kale raised in cedar boxes between the SkyTrain
pillars. The propinquity of corn along boulevards.
A dream of zero emissions for the wheat leaning
beside highways. And from the rooftops, fields
next to airstrips. Golf courses. Freedom Space
Station Grow-ops and the back of a Dodge Ram.

Bush beans between parking plazas. Schoolyard
potatoes and pumpkins. More food and flowers
for Hastings Street. Bees on the block. Biosphere
plums on university farms. Apple trees espaliered
beside bike lanes. Carrot bins behind bus stops.
Backyard chickens. The alley where I planted
the raspberries two years ago. They were picked
while I slept.

THE GARBAGE TRUCK TRASHED
THE SUNFLOWER

It had just overtaken the fence, springing colour
over the slotted, grey-flecked cedar boards
that enclosed the small yard and garden.

I imagine its big head hit with a *thwunk*
on the lane of compacted gravel and dirt.
Of course, nobody heard it, and chances are

nobody even saw what were the pincer-like
hydraulic arms side-swiping the giant stalk
during the dust-up of high-pitched stops

and starts forking from bin to bin. I don't
blame the driver—there isn't much time
to collect all that garbage. What's the life

of one sunflower? Sure, I planted it there
and it grew heavy-headed until it leaned out
into the lane a little, but I didn't want to tie it

to the fence. Besides, a magnum opus of sun-
flower centres the yard like a tuba's high note
blasting the brightest yellow of the year.

The six-foot stalk stands straight against gravity,
but its hunched neck bends as if it'll break
under the weight of its seeded head peering

onto sweet peas, salad blooms and the carrot
frills that dance in the gentle breeze. For some
time now, people have been asking questions

about it. Though the end is certain, the sun will
only shine through the spindles of red maple
that way this time. The fractured light will stay

on the gold band of petals like fire-licks only
so long. If I look long enough, I feel happy,
even laugh. And the light has changed already.

AT THE CURB ON GRAVELEY STREET

Dominic tells me dandelion leaves are best
picked before the yellow flowers go to seed,

before their grey globes blow off with cotton-
wood pollens, pollution, and dust. He pinches

a sprig from the full basket on his red walker.
I smell only creosote from the telephone pole.

He says, "You have to wash each leaf, boil,
rinse, change the water, boil and wash again.

Stir in garlic, chickpeas, parmesan and pasta.
Open windows! What could be better?" Across

the street, Marcello ties a bouquet of calla lilies
to the cherry tree where Maria died. A black

truck. Rain at dusk. He cried with so much of
his body. Still, years later, he works the garden

to feed more families. This morning he found
handfuls of mushrooms up at the park to mix

with lettuce larger than a large person's head.
Dominic says, people move through this city

as if it were a machine. He shakes my hand
into a tight fist. Two doors up, Ting-Mie ties

together broken hockey sticks into an obelisk
for her broad beans. I wave to her and wonder

how much exhaust has blown into the house.

NEIGHBOUR

On the street lined by bare chestnut trees
like the shackled hands of giants, a teenager

stoops to write inside the crosswalk's white lines.
His blue hood falls back off his stubble of hair

as he leaps as quick as the horn of the Ford F-150.
What's next? Even the STOP HARPER sign is tagged

in mangled English, Hebrew, Arabic, or who knows
what. Who will say the words? *Shalom, Salaam,*

Hello. As I get closer, I realize that he is scrubbing
letters off the street while his two friends kick

a green bucket by the curb. The one I know smiles
and says, "Busted." I smile back. He's my neighbour.

CLOWNING AROUND IN THE GARDEN

You thought the peppers would thrive in the direct sun
this year, but they did not. You toss the shrivelled ones

onto the compost. The zucchinis are ready. Last year you
tried them grilled, baked, fried, and raw. Picasso trundles

up the path. His feet swing to the sides with each big step.
He says, "Art is this moment and the next." He is akimbo

when you tell him it's close. He rolls a zucchini on the grass.
He says, "People want to find a meaning in everything." You

remember *Two Women Running on the Beach*. They splashed
into the water and they floated their breasts. You think, "A rose

is a rose is a rose." You climb the ladder to pick what is left
of the grapes, and you see the scratch marks from the raccoon

that plundered the vine last night. You look for the tennis shoe
you threw from the window. You see your copy of *Hamlet*.

Up there, the hot sun on your neck, you sing: If I could fit
into a sky-blue harlequin, I would swing, swing, and swing!

GALLERY WALK

Blackberries in a basket. Emily squishes
a ripe one onto the canvas.

Cedars set the backdrop. The crooked stair
sinks as you step onto it.

The door is locked. There are no windows.
Water drips off the bowers

onto overlapping stages. Pinnacles of light
breach the canopy. The forest is

shading. You move closer to the thick paint.
The undergrowth whispers

in the chilling wind. *Keep going. And keep.*
And so you do. The church rots

in the splendour of the forest. Black is the night,
sweet is the blackberry.

MOUTH

As I breathe in the salty air, the wind makes
the sound sing off my windbreaker. Air traffic
roars, sandpipers eep, and underneath, the river
regurgitates. A heron, hunched on a piling, rises
over the Fraser's north arm choked by log boom
after log boom after hollow-hulled barges heaped
with woodchips. Greasy grasses grow through
drift, and a diesel engine. The sky and the ocean
hold grey to grey, but the horizon's line is definite.
The mist rolls, and dissipates. A cloud separates.
Sunlight flashes off the chops like so many stars
shining and dying. Waves curl up and collapse.
A water bottle skids in the wash. Flies hover over
froths of sea foam. Gelatinous. I leash the dog.
The Fraser drains. All the things we have put in
our bodies. The tide comes in, goes out.

THE BEST DIFFERENCES

The chunk of ice
in the shape of
a horse or a ploughshare;
nevertheless, it broke
into the river,
hung up on a boulder,
and eventually became
the best of what
we are—cold, clear
and warming up.

And of the which,
and the everywhere,
there are the children.

Our younger son,
balancing the one L
in his name to walk
around the perimeter
of the high fence.
No fear. I had none
as he was smooth,
steady, like ice melting.

And our older son, as we
walked on the wet sand
at low tide, the clams
spitting water. He already

digging with his hands,
while we talked
of getting the shovel.

TRIGONOMETRY

The morning of my son's first hockey practice,
a crow woke me on its way west. Its call
in the dark, a bed spring. Awake like a wire,
I watched my son on the mirror of ice. His skates
stiff, he pushed off, turned on loose ankles,
twirled to his knees. Outside, the sunrise,
a long thin band through maples. He said he fell
too often. I said not to worry, skates loosen.

My wife was at the door. *David's dead.*
A bomb. A man on a bicycle.
                              David giving
out candy? What kind?
                         Candy. It matters.
All of it
          a feather.

          What the army can take.
                              I want
reasons. These bursts of momentum. The crow
that morning. First from the roost. Like my son,
like David. And this damn wondering if crows
react to light before we do.

THE LAST ONION IN THE WICKER BASKET

When he peels it, the space
under his thumbnail fills with skin.
It crunches as he cuts it in half. Outside,
rain pools on the acrylic deck.
The light over the sink. The picture
of his son swinging in a pike position
on the hawthorn.

He slides one half closer. Slices. A rock skips
on the surface of a lake. Rings expand.
A sluice opens. His nose tingling,
I will not cry. He repeats,

but the second half falls apart. His eye,
his left eye. He washes
the knife with his hand.
Because he cannot find a towel,
he uses his pants.

A cell phone vibrates. His older son cackles
in the living room.
The butter.

THE LEAF

A deep breath or two before walking up
to the podium will help you to relax,
but it may also make you feel like a leaf,
its base breaking from its stem. Face it
when the hand, or worse, the leg starts,
and you feel light and then heavy, almost
a part of the ground, you know you will
be headed that way anyway. Statuesque?
A statue doesn't shake, even if it had been
sculpted to suggest a changing attitude,
or with volumes to impose depth, or frailty.
Some people can speak as if they were
cartwheeling or twirling or even whispering
to the person beside them on the bus
just as they would to ten or a million. Yes,
sometimes I can. It's easy. And sometimes,
like maybe right now, it's not. I am falling
like the leaf that has run out of sap, detached,
wavering, turning, and maybe, even briefly,
because of wind, rising. If I say it doesn't
matter, it does. If I say I'm alive, have some
courage—just have fun, you have kids—
still there is the leaf. And however beautiful,
slow, or quick its descent, when it touches
the ground, it makes a sound. And yet most
of the time, it's inaudible to the human ear.

STAYING GROUNDED

After a heaping defeat, it is best, at least
I've heard, to get a good sleep, to leave
the party early—but after dancing, to rise
as the sun brightens the blinds. Still I prefer
walking on the soft shores at Lost Lagoon
where the feathery festoons allow for frivolity,
and the fragility of old men feeding raccoons
French fries allows for perspective on loss.
Over in the inner harbour, water is skinned
by sleek-armed rowers whose co-operation
should be example enough. And beyond that,
new leaves shimmer on Deadman's Island
where the Salish battled, and raised some
of their dead high into cedars, where Chinese
men built homes from which they were evicted,
and where the military persists. Anyone can
lose anything at any time. And these words
are not a matter of life or death or shelter or
what will determine the next time I roast
a chicken with rosemary for remembrance,
which is a good enough reason not to apply
for the one-way expedition to Mars. Maybe
if it could be with my wife, whose lips can
part the skies, but she'd tire of my brooding,
and we'd have to set the boundaries on another
planet, so maybe not without the chickadee's
two clear notes I heard early this morning,
or the swallows that swung their wide circles
around me by the darkening lake at dusk.

I DON'T KNOW

The gull hiccups around the purple starfish
in its throat. Its head half-cocked to sky,
yellow-ringed eyes fixed, and stick legs stock-
still on the parapet, it seems unconcerned
that I, and a woman wearing a green raincoat,
stand a step away. At first I think, stupid bird.
You scavenger in a feathered frock. Then I worry
that it'll die right in front of us. How does one
pull a starfish out of a seagull? The hard spines
on skin, cartilage and hollow bone. If I tried to
save either I'd surely kill both, so I just stand
there and stare, until the woman snaps a picture
and says, "Must be the boa-power of gulls."

SCAPE

The garden's Salvador Dali. An invitation
to an early supper. You marvel at his thin, horsehair
paintbrush, his exacting flair with his moustache. You set
down the Pinot gris. A fresh cut tomato sprinkled
with pepper. You say, it's the Irish way. He says,
all the salt in Almeria. You take a bite as you look out
at the Mediterranean. It shimmers. Fresh sheets on a long line.
You think, Jesus must have also looked people in the eye.
That the oceans allow for the roots of this world. Glaciers.
You twirl the bulb. Mint leaves on the endive,
the olives glisten. Still, sleep is near. He smiles
as you bite down on the scape. Garlic light, a zinger
of onion, clove. Your mouth warm all the way back
to the village. The moon rises red from the water.
This will not be the last supper. Every five minutes
together, a new world.

AIR CONDITIONER

The river rived the land and flowed
1375 kilometres from its headwaters
of 100% visibility to none. It carved
valleys into bent knees and elbows
that carried 17 million tonnes of silt
to the blooming delta where the salmon
spawned or did not spawn. Fishermen
waited or did not wait; the river had
cooled in its perpetuity and spread out
to the ocean. Again the magic of water
rose up and up to be counted on. To be
counted on? River it to me. Press on.
Please press on.

ACKNOWLEDGEMENTS

The first epigraph is from David Suzuki's *The Legacy* (Greystone Books, 2010). The second epigraph is from Sina Queyras's poem "Even the Idea of River" in *Lemon Hound* (Coach House Books, 2006). "Reading Rilke on Dog Mountain" is inspired by "Parting" from Rilke's *New Poems* translated by Edward Snow (North Point Press, 2001). The reference to "In a Foreign Park" is from the same volume. The quoted line in "Finn's Slough" is from John Steinbeck's *Cannery Row* (Penguin Books, 1992). "The Theatre of the Absurd" reference in "The Accident" is from Stephen Hume's article in *The Vancouver Sun*, December 19, 2013. The "rose is ..." reference in "Clowning Around in the Garden" is after Gertrude Stein's iconic phrase.

"Dedication" is in the memory of Derek Miller.

Earlier versions of some of these poems have appeared in *Canadian Literature, CV2, Existere, The Fiddlehead, PRISM international, subTerrain,* and *The Montreal Global Anthology.* Many thanks to their editors.

I am thankful for the Vancouver Library, Central Branch. I spent much time writing there. Thank you to Jami Macarty for her teachings. Thanks to Ray Guraliuk for the directions. Thanks to Mia Wood for the generosity. Special thanks to Zsuzsi Gartner for her incisive reading. Many thanks to the staff at Anvil. To Karen and Shazia. And to Brian Kaufman. You are! And forever thank you to Susan, Chris, and Wil.

ABOUT THE AUTHOR

Jeff Steudel's poetry has appeared in several publications including *PRISM international, CV2, The Fiddlehead, subTerrain,* and *Canadian Literature.* He has received the Ralph Gustafson Poetry Prize, and his work was chosen as a finalist for the CBC Literary Awards. *Foreign Park* is his first book of poetry. He lives in Vancouver.